| ARS EDENDI |

R.B.C. Huygens

ARS EDENDI

A practical introduction
to editing medieval Latin texts

BREPOLS

D/2000/0095/124
ISBN 2-503-51162-7

Quotiens scribes aliquid quod editurus es, scito morum tuorum te hominibus chirographum dare.

Ps.–Seneca *De moribus*,
ed. Haase, 1902, p. 65, no. 130.

The following abbreviations have been used:
CCCM = Corpus Christianorum, *Continuatio mediae-
valis*. – CSEL = Corpus scriptorum ecclesiasticorum lati-
norum. – MGH = Monumenta Germaniae Historica (*AA*:
Auctores antiquissimi).
The following titles have been quoted:
*Accessus ad auctores, Bernard d'Utrecht, Conrad d'Hirsau:
Dialogus super auctores*, 1970. – *Monumenta Vizeliacensia*
[Annals, Cartulary and Chronicle of Vézelay, see below,
note 123], CCCM 42, 1976. – Bernard of Utrecht,
Commentum in Theodolum, 1977. – *Le moine Idung*
[Idungus of Prüfening] *et ses deux ouvrages: 'Argumentum
super quatuor questionibus' et 'Dialogus duorum mona-
chorum'*, 1980. – *Apologiae duae* [Gozechin, *Epistola ad
Walcherum*, and Burchard of Bellevaux, *Apologia de barbis*], CCCM 72, 1985. – William of Tyre, *Chronicle*, CCCM
63 and 63A, 1986. – Berengar of Tours, *Rescriptum contra
Lanfrannum*, CCCM 84, 1988. – Guibert of Nogent: *La
tradition manuscrite de Guibert de Nogent*, Steenbrugge
1991 (Instrumenta Patristica XXI), *De (sanctis et eorum)
pigneribus*, CCCM 127, 1993, and *Dei gesta per Francos*,
CCCM 127A, 1996. – *Peregrinationes tres* [Saewulf, John
of Würzburg, Theoderic], CCCM 139, 1994. – *Serta = Serta
mediaevalia, textus varii saeculorum X-XIII*, CCCM 171
and 171A, 2000.

THIS BOOKLET, IT SHOULD BE STATED FROM THE OUT-SET, has not the pretension to do anything but what its title suggests: to serve as a kind of practical guide for those who want to edit medieval Latin writings, but who lack the experience. It is by no means going to resemble anything like a systematic treatment of textual criticism. That would require a much more detailed discussion. What I am offering are a few practical, maybe occasionally somewhat unorthodox recommendations for editing Latin texts which were written during the Middle Ages. I should like to emphasize this restriction. Even if many problems are fundamentally the same, classical and patristic texts each present different aspects: if certain observations should be more widely applicable, so much the better.

The following pages are based on many years' familiarity with manuscripts and the Latin texts which are their *raison d'être*. They contain personal views and advice. Some of these may seem to be obvious. Whoever feels that way should recall St Matthew's word *non est opus valentibus medicus, sed male haben-*

tibus[1] – but if the *valentes* were really numerous, the
number of failed editions would be considerably
lower. Although no single problem is going to be dealt
with for which not many more examples might be
given, I had to make choices, in accordance with
Horace's wise precept: *quidquid praecipies, esto bre-
vis, ut cito dicta / percipiant animi dociles teneantque
fideles.* A few (I hope well chosen) examples may each
time suffice to illustrate my point, and with only a few
exceptions these have been taken from a number of
my own editions[2]. They won't act as a safeguard
against making any mistakes – we all make them. But
they may hopefully help to avoid at least some before
an edition is printed, by suggesting methods and sig-
nalling pitfalls: *septies cadet iustus, et resurget.*

I start from the assumption that readers are familiar with basic manuals, bibliographical guides, methods and theories. Especially works on general
principles are only too well represented on the mar-
ket... I should not, at least not for beginners, recommend Paul Maas's well-known *Textkritik/Textual
Criticism* (1958) which deals exclusively with classical Latin and Greek texts and which, though valuable, is rather dogmatic; but I whole-heartedly
subscribe to Ludwig Bieler's pages on 'The
Grammarian's Craft – an Introduction to Textual

1. See p. 48.
2. See the list on p. 6.

Criticism'[3]. We all know what would be ideal: it is the modest aim of this booklet to assist in making the best of our not seldom scant resources, in order to produce well thought-out editions.

Editing texts is an art. And as with all arts, you have to be at least moderately talented, or you will be a failure. The talents you do have can be developed, indeed will definitely be developed through exercise and practice. This is a time consuming process. I'll come back to this aspect later. But first two fundamental questions have to be asked, and answered, if you want to edit a text: why *should* you, and why should *you*? You *should*, because the work is essential, as most of our knowledge of material and intellectual life in the period we are concerned with here is exclusively based on written testimony. The more we have this information made available in print, and the more accurately this is done, the better much larger groups other than just specialists will be able to study all aspects of ages past. At the same time, an editor of medieval Latin texts should not fail to keep in touch with archaeology: it is too bad to print the word *gladius*, *ensis* or *spatha* in your text without ever having seen such a weapon dating from the period that particular text deals with, and I for one felt really embarrassed, while editing the 12th cen-

3. *Classica Folia*, published by The Catholic Classical Association of Greater New York, [5]1965.

tury *Apologia de barbis*, when I proved unable to trace any razor which the author of that wonderful treatise might himself have observed being used.

But why should *you*? The answer is: because, although you'll only gradually fully develop your talents, you are confident that you are already well prepared. Now are you really? If you are not, your edition is bound to turn out a bad edition. A bad edition is not necessarily a useless one[4], but it remains an unreliable one, and just as a thing of beauty is a joy for ever, an unsatisfactory edition is a long lasting annoyance. So let me assist you in discovering whether you are suited to become an editor or not. On no account should you think that in order to be one it is enough to have a computer, be able to read a manuscript and know sufficient Latin to understand what the text is about. You have to be painstakingly accurate – and, incidentally, do not expect to be praised for this because, in the words of A.E. Housman, accuracy is a duty and not a virtue; and though it may be true that absolute perfection is not attainable on earth, you should not resign yourself to that sorry fact but strive to be as good as possible. In this field nothing is gained by observing the main lines whilst simultaneously blurring the picture by overlooking the numerous small, often bothersome details which accompany the editing of a text. Know your limita-

4. See *Peregrinationes tres*, pp.18-19.

tions, avoid texts which do not really interest you or which are beyond your capacities: you do not have to be a monk to publish a monastic text, nor a poet to edit poetry, but if you do not have a feeling for metrics, stick to prose and do not publish verse, if philosophy is not your cup of tea, then leave philosophical texts to others, and if you are not familiar with the geography of the Near East, abstain from editing (and even translating) texts dealing with the Crusader States[5]. And if you do not know the Bible, don't edit any text at all without first having thoroughly familiarized yourself with the typical flavour of biblical language. If you only know the Bible in your own language, start reading it more than once in Latin. Although there are concordances which I myself use frequently (of which Peultier's is one of the best), they don't make up for ignorance, and any-

5. *Peregrinationes tres*, pp.18-19 (as in note 4), and below, page 59; to quote but one more example: in R. Levine's translation of Guibert of Nogent's *Dei gesta per Francos* (below, note 110), the *Portus Sancti Symeonis*, Antioch's harbour, some 20 miles SW of the city, has consistently been made to be one of its gates... Of course, the same holds good with regard to texts concerning European affairs, especially those that mention many smaller localities: in the Chronicle of Vézelay, Arnulfus de Ferrariis was not called after Ferrara in Italy but after one of the many Ferrières, Amicus de Ulmo after Lormes (l'orme), and Meschinus de Nancapra after... Nanchèvre ! See also the Introduction to those same *Monumenta Vizeliacensia*, on the *Portus Sancti Ayoli*, p. XVIII, note 16.

way, to get the right answer one has to know how to ask the right question: so many phrases, even in the most unbiblical context, owe at least something to the Vulgate, that you should be able to intuitively recognize their unmistakable ring. Although it is true that many a formula does not come directly from the Vulgate or, by way of memory, even indirectly, but from Liturgy, a thorough familiarity with that Vulgate is a prerequisite I cannot insist upon enough. It is indeed surprising how much the Vulgata has influenced medieval Latin, not only by means of grammatical constructions and through direct quotations, but by its implicit use as well, the treacherous frequency of which often plays tricks even on editors who know their Bible inside out. William of Tyre, while describing the Crusader envoys as being very impressed by the splendour of the caliph's court (19, 19, 14), makes them watch the muslim ruler appear *revelata facie* – words taken from 2 Cor. 3, 18, where the text speaks of those who will behold the glory of the Lord! In the *Epistola ad heremitas*[6], in an explicit quotation from one of Seneca's Letters, the original words are replaced by the wording of St Matthew 8, 19. Who would suspect that such an innocent indication of the spring: *eo tempore quo solent reges ad bella procedere*, is derived from 2 Kings 11, 1, or the poetical *sibilum aurae tenuis*[7] from 3 Kings 19, 12?

6. *Serta*, p. 217, 50-52.
7. *Ad heremitas* (as in note 6: p.216), 41-42.

Guibert of Nogent, mentioning the lavish wedding of the daughter of French King Philip I, writes *fecit apud Carnotum* [Chartres] *eius nuptias in magna gloria*[8], even this seemingly factual account being based on the Bible, viz. 1 Macc. 10, 58: *et dedit ei... filiam suam et fecit nuptias eius Ptolemaidae, sicut reges in magna gloria*. And in another work of this same author, the only complete manuscript presents... *quod Iudeis* metum *fidelium impresumptibile erat*[9]. All editors, as well as a 17th century copy emended this to *metu*, which from a strictly grammatical point of view[10] makes perfect sense. One should, however, maintain the reading *metum*, but make it depend upon *<propter>*[11]: Guibert undoubtedly had the formula with which St John[12] describes the exact opposite situation in mind, viz. the *fideles* being on their guard *propter metum Iudaeorum*! If the first editor of the poet Gillebert had known his Bible at all, he would not have printed *condemnavit perfidis rex superbam vasti* (a line which, being nonsense, he should not have printed anyway), but *condempnavit Persidis rex superbam Vasti* (Esther 1, 9-22)[13]; and if one of my own compatriots had known his Bible bet-

---

8. *Dei gesta per Francos* 7,1844-1846.
9. *Monodiae* (Autobiographie), ed.Labande, Paris 1981, p.424, 12-13; see *Serta*, p. 311, note 1.
10. See p. 52.
11. For the sign < > , see p. 62.
12. Chapters 7,13 and 19,38, and again 20,19.
13. Gillebert II, 48,4 (*Serta*, p. 749).

ter, he would not have read in some 14th century manuscript: *iste sunt due sorores luxurie: colla et oliba*, explaining (?) these words as 'la coule' (a monk's frock) and the olive (*oliva*)[14], but instead as the two whores Oolla and Ooliba mentioned in Ezekiel (23, 4-44). *Omnia munda mundis*, but an editor should not make such blunders.

As for Latin Liturgy, that is as complicated a source as it is an important one, and this complexity is baffling not only to non-Catholics! Unfortunately, since the Church has largely dropped the use of Latin, even in monastic communities the number of people who know liturgical formulas by heart, and might thus be able to initiate you into them and help you out with them, is steadily decreasing. One example may suffice. When Gerald of Fleury[15] addressed the Virgin Mary as follows: *Tu cunctas hereses perimis virtute <perhenni>*, he clearly drew from the same source as Guibert of Nogent in his *Contra iudaizantem et Iudeos*, where the abbot says: *Certe credideramus hactenus, quia legeramus, virginem illam unicam... in universo mundo interemisse pravitates hereticas*[16]. Medieval readers hardly needed the reminder *quia legeramus*; for modern readers it is a helpful one, in that it points to a source. But to identify this source (an antiphone)

14. P.C. Boeren, *Twee Maaslandse dichters in dienst van Karel de Stoute*, 1968, p. 56, note 16.
15. *Serta*, p. 683 (III,57).
16. *Serta*, p. 318, 67-69.

our post-Tridentine missals are of no use, and to trace it in Dom R.-J. Hesbert's *Corpus antiphonalium Officii* one has to know the first words (*Gaude, Maria virgo*)...

Regarding the patristic sources of medieval Latin texts, this is an immense field which, I should mention to say, is nevertheless easier to become acquainted with than with Liturgy. Several of the most widely used authors were also among the most prolific ones, and the fact that in the later Middle Ages much patristic lore did not come directly from its source but from florilegia and from ubiquitous canonical collections such as Ivo of Chartres' and Gratian's *Decretum* does not make things any easier. Not every striking formula in medieval Latin has been derived from an earlier source: if this were the case, it would make reading hardly worth while at all. You nonetheless have to be prepared for this; and naturally you have to be thoroughly at home in classical Latin literature in the first place. Certain authors were more widely admired and used than others, and reached peaks in their popularity in different centuries[17]. Some were hardly known, while others, to make at least something easier, were not known at all. But one thing is certain: the better you know your classics, the better you are equipped to deal with medieval Latin texts. It would also be most helpful if you knew the

17. (cf. note 62) See the note on Naso (Ovid) in *Serta*, p.804, note 5.

vernacular language of the author of the Latin text you are dealing with. In spite of its supranational character, medieval Latin was nobody's mother tongue, and many a baffling construction, expression or pun can be explained by translating it back into the author's vernacular: it may not always be as striking as in the case of General Sir Charles Napier, who allegedly summarized the success of his Indian campaign (1843) in one single word: *peccavi* ('I have Sind')[18], but all the same... When dealing with a text like the *Reynardus Vulpes*, the Latin adaptation of a Flemish original, the point is obvious[19]. But time and again, unclassical words and constructions pop up in all kinds of other works as well, which can (not infrequently only) be explained by the native language in which the author continued to think while writ-

18. E. Thompson and G.T. Garratt, *Rise and Fulfilment of British Rule in India*, 1935, p. 359; G. Moorhouse, *India Britannica*, 1983, p. 19; Wendy Doniger, *"I have Scinde": Flogging a Dead (White Male Orientalist) Horse*, in *The Journal of Asian Studies* 58, 1999, pp. 940-943 (960).

19. *Serta*, pp. 817-885. In lines 1272-1274, the cunning fox is pleading for his life while dangling before the eyes of King Lion, who is as stupid as he is greedy, the vision of an imaginary treasure: ...*plurima gaza iacet/hic Ermerici selle, gemme, dyadema, / regia septra* (sic) *iacent, aurea vasa simul*. We do not know what kind of manuscript of his Flemish model Baldwin used, or exactly how he used it. But from the word *selle* it is clear that he read *trone* (thrones), and not *crone* (crowns) which is the reading of all the (considerably younger) extant Flemish manuscripts.

ing Latin. John of Würzburg noticed the (*pinnas vel*) *cinnas*, meaning the battlements, thus creating the word *cinn(a)e*, hereby latinizing, according to his German pronunciation, *Zinnen*[20]. And Guibert of Nogent writes *hostis* when he refers to, not the enemy, but the troops, the army as such (*l'ost*)[21]. Personally I would go so far as to signal, but not correct, grammatical errors such as *arbor... quem* (*un* arbre, *der* Baum) or *color... quam* (*la* couleur, *die* Farbe), as long as they can be explained by the author's mother tongue[22].

Do not make too early or too ambitious a start – that's hardly how success will come your way. On the other hand, if you wait too long you will become old without having acquired the necessary experience in this particular field. So begin with short texts, and such as will attract the general interest: not everything that has remained unpublished, or has been bungled by some previous editor, is worth your while simply because it is written in Latin. Starting with short texts has several advantages: you will more easily and more often attract the attention of scholars to whom it is to your advantage to become known to, than if you spend the same amount of time on one

---

20. *Peregrinationes tres*, p. 90,274.
21. *Dei gesta per Francos* 4,439, also 6,169 and 719. See also above, note 5.
22. See also p. 42.

single, much longer text; also, it will enable you to acquire experience and develop your own techniques, because, apart from the problems all texts have in common, each of them will present difficulties of its own you will have to learn to cope with; and if, in spite of all your efforts, you yourself or others should be discontented with a work once it has been published, a short text can more easily be done over again, whereas a long one will inevitably remain a stain upon your record for a much longer period.

Do not prepare more than one edition at a time, concentrate on one only, and you will master its various aspects twice as well: however vast your knowledge and, ultimately, your experience, preparing an edition is quite different from preparing a study on some general subject. Once you are involved in it, don't be afraid of making a decision or a statement you may be criticized for: none of us is infallible, the point is not so much whether you are right or should have decided otherwise, but whether you are capable of doing the work you are doing. Editors who are too anxious about taking the risk a choice between readings inevitably presents, should abstain altogether or restrict themselves to publishing what they think are autographs – and even then they will have to cut several knots.

But *is* that particular manuscript really an autograph? Be careful here, just as careful as you have to be when it comes to attributing an anonymous text to some author or other. Though different, both problems have something in common which is both necessary and simple to keep in mind: there are always more candidates than you may be prepared to admit. We know the handwriting of some authors quite well: Florus of Lyons, John the Scot, Ademar of Chabannes, Sigebert of Gembloux, Lambert of St Omer (*Liber Floridus*) or St Thomas Aquinas, for instance. But on the whole you have to be extremely cautious when it comes to pronouncing a manuscript an autograph[23], and thus to debase, if not eliminate, all other manuscripts of the same text[24]: one should start from the assumption that one is *not* dealing with an autograph unless there is compelling evidence to the contrary. To pronounce a manuscript to be written in the author's hand is ultimately a decision a philologist, not a palaeographer, has to make, and it must be based on internal evidence. As an editor of medieval Latin texts you naturally have to be thoroughly familiar with palaeography, and evidence from both disciplines must of course be used to corroborate your conclusions. But since it cannot be denied that at any given time always more than just one man was able to

23. From the list of authors whose autographs are said to have been preserved, I emphatically exclude Ralph the Bald (Raoul Glaber) (cf. *Deutsches Archiv* 46, 1990, pp.601-602), Berengar of Tours and Guibert of Nogent. Also, C.H. Beeson's book (1930) on *Lupus of Ferrières as scribe and text critic* [of Cicero's *De oratore*] does not contain even the slightest proof of the assumption that we are indeed dealing with an autograph. See also p. 46.
24. See also pp. 29-30.

write, the final word lies with the philologist. And one more warning: the fact that there are no scribal errors in your manuscript's text is in itself no proof that you are dealing with an autograph, which may actually contain as many of them as you are yourself likely to make in writing out any significant piece of work[25].

You have to be no less cautious when it comes to attributing anonymously transmitted texts to known authors. You are on no less slippery ground here than you are in accepting, or challenging, a manuscript's attribution. If texts in manuscripts do bear an author's name, one will have to check if the attribution is correct, or may be correct. There are many authors, such as St Jerome, Bede, Hrabanus Maurus, Remigius of Auxerre[26] or Bernard of Clairvaux, whose names inspired such confidence that lots of texts, which they would never even have thought of composing, were attributed to them, because many a scribe could not, or would not, resist the temptation to mask anonymous – or his own – writings with more famous names, and thus try to enhance their credibility or assure their very survival. In this respect such scribes were not fundamentally different from many philologists of more recent times, who likewise did not give up before they had added an anonymous text they had found to the

25. Even the original *Bundesbrief*, the venerable birth-certificate of Switserland (1291), is not free from scribal errors!
26. Cf. *Serta*, pp. 25-33(55): "Lettres attribuées à Remi d'Auxerre".

list of writings of well-known authors. Consciously or subconsciously, vanity plays its role here: it is nicer to have one's name associated with famous than with obscure writers, and if one has to lend, then better to the rich. Other criteria lacking, I think one may assume that the manuscript attribution to a certain author becomes more plausible if this author was less well known at the time, or at the place where the manuscript was written, and there is certainly little ground not to accept, be it with a reservation, what you cannot really prove to be wrong. I am also inclined to lend more credence to long and explicit headings and attributions[27]. However, as really objective criteria are usually lacking, don't play Oedipus, don't be afraid to admit you don't know, always remember that many people knew how to compose a text (or even without knowing, did so), that expressions may have been more common than you are aware of, and that, not infrequently, ideas were just in the air.

Let us go back to the moment you have decided to edit a text which is not a charter or a collection of charters. I stress this point, since charters are an altogether different matter which requires a different approach. Just keep in mind however, that the way you edit charters for their own sake, either as isolated documents or as part of a cartulary or other diplomatic collection, is not the same as publishing them

27. Cf. *Serta*, p. 94 and pp. 232-235; Guibert of Nogent, *Dei gesta per Francos*, p.39 and note 51.

as part of a narrative text in which they have been inserted to support or explain the context[28]. Let us now assume you started looking for manuscripts: manuscripts which have already been used in previous editions or are mentioned in the literature[29]; manuscripts hitherto unnoticed or unused; and, in the case of a text you believe to have discovered yourself, other manuscripts than the one in which you stumbled upon your find. In this last case you will first have to try to ascertain whether the discovery really *is* yours. When one considers a text to be unpublished, this means nothing else than that one does not remember ever having seen that text either in manuscript or in print, or mentioned in the available repertories. Such a thing happens quite often, since the field one is presumed to master is a vast one. If such a text is considered worth publishing (do ask yourself if it is!), the first thing to do is to make sure it has really remained unpublished. Unfortunately, to do so is easier said than done, because quite a substantial part of medieval Latin literature is hidden in rare books or in periodicals not accessible everywhere, and even the number of repertories of first words (*incipits*) is disappointingly small[30]. There is,

28. In that case, avoid the capital A for a siglum, since diplomatists use it to indicate originals. See also note 112.
29. See p. 66.
30. It may be hard to find a text in an incipitarium if your manuscript omits the beginning. So do not restrict your search to the very first words only.

of course, the invaluable Institut de Recherche et d'Histoire des Textes in Paris; much is now also available on CD-Rom, but equally much is not (yet), especially texts published in the indigestibly large collections of texts of Martène and Durand, d'Achery, Pez and Mabillon. Certainly, there are also helpful colleagues. *Sed quis custodiet ipsos custodes*? Even the best informed scholar is not omniscient, and proof, if at all needed, of this sad admission is the publication by so renowned a palaeographer as the late Bernhard Bischoff, in his *Anecdota novissima* (1984), of an incomplete commentary on the Lord's Prayer, which the heading presents as *expositiones Berengarii*, and Bischoff (pp. 49-56) as an ineditum of Berengar of Tours[31]. The second part of the text, however, has nothing to do with (this) Berengar, whereas the first part is merely the beginning of the *Confessio* of Berengar's contemporary, and opponent (!), Guitmund of Aversa, which has long since been printed in Migne's Patrology (149, 1495-1497A)[32]. Also, shortly before World War II, Dom Alban Dold, an important Benedictine scholar, discovered, and prepared for printing, some fragments he wanted to publish in the equally important Revue Bénédictine; but before doing so, he very wisely tried to ascertain if they were really unknown to the learned world. There was no better way of doing this than by ask-

31. See also *Serta*, pp. 234-235.
32. Fr. Dolbeau, *Revue des études latines* 63, 1985, p. 305.

ing Dom Germain Morin, one of the most brilliant patristic scholars of recent times. Dom Morin answered the request, and the answer, which was published in the introduction to the texts in question, is worth quoting (my translation): "I am satisfied I can assure you that nowhere have I found the slightest trace of these texts, not even where they should have been mentioned almost necessarily, and so you may safely assume they are still unpublished. These fragments really deserve to be published …", etc. Who would be in any doubt, seeing his own conviction confirmed in such a way by such a famous scholar? Unfortunately, both Dold *and* Morin overlooked the fact that seventeen years earlier Dom Morin himself had already published the very same texts in the same Revue Bénédictine, from the same Vienna manuscript in which his fellow-Benedictine Alban Dold had just rediscovered them …[33] You always have to search for additional manuscripts, and even though you may not find what you are really looking for, in one way or

33. *Revue Bénédictine* 51, 1939, pp. 122-138 (137) and 34, 1922, pp. 265-275; Dom E. Dekkers, *Clavis Patrum Latinorum* (³1995), pp. 257-258, no.755. A few months before his death (12 February 1946) Dom Morin himself confessed: "Malheureusement (…), les circonstances me mettant dans l'impossibilité de dresser une bibliographie même incomplète de mes nombreux travaux... dont souvent j'ai perdu moi-même le souvenir" (G. Gheysens and P.-P Verbraken, *La carrière scientifique de dom Germain Morin (1861-1946)*, Steenbrugge 1986 (Instrumenta Patristica XV), p. 80.

another your quest will always be rewarded. Even
while only superficially studying medieval Latin literature, time and again one comes across authors
whose productivity originally resulted in more works
than we now know, and, the other way round, across
many texts for which no author is mentioned at all.
The great number of texts – classical, patristic and
medieval – preserved in, or known from, just one
manuscript makes us realize how much we owe to
pure chance, or have sheer bad luck to blame for[34].
The fact that quite a few texts, which we know to have
been written, have still not been discovered cannot
be explained exclusively by the unimaginable losses
incurred during the many centuries which followed
their appearance; it is also due to the relatively small
number of people who really do look for them. Those
who do, see their search severely hampered by the
fact that a large number of manuscripts have only
very inadequately been catalogued or even not at all,
or because they are found in collections to which one
has no, or only limited, access, or because of the ever
increasing cost of photocopies and visits to far-away
libraries and the lack of funds available for this kind

---

34. *Serta*, p. 414, Berengar, *Rescriptum*, p. 9, *Apologiae duae*,
   p. 4 (Gozechin) and pp. 130-131 (*Apologia de barbis*), etc.;
   J. Stengers, *Réflexions sur le manuscrit unique, ou un aspect
   du hasard en histoire*, in *Scriptorium* 40, 1986, pp. 54-80
   (cf. H. Silvestre, *Bulletin de théologie ancienne et médiévale*
   1987, p. 196, no. 423). See also p. 26.

of activity, and also because many a librarian has a tendency to look upon visitors as if they were potential pilferers, thus managing to turn the journey to his treasure-house into something resembling a journey to Canossa. Under such circumstances it can never be excluded, even in the case of well-known and thoroughly researched authors, that a text which is considered lost is in fact still awaiting discovery and better days to come[35]. So don't abandon the search for manuscripts and texts until you are satisfied you really have attempted all you possibly could. Never forget either that if a text is worth publishing, it is worth having its whole manuscript tradition researched. Apart from that, the more manuscripts you find, the easier it becomes to establish how much, and by whom, a text was really read, and why, and to which group of people (e.g. Cistercians of the Ile-de-France, Benedictines of Southern England) an author may have owed his influence or even his very survival[36]. If you are able to establish such things, you have at the same time made a contribution to the intellectual history of the Middle Ages. It may also reveal that a text *we* qualify as important may hardly have been read at all at the time of which it is deemed such an important witness.

35. Cf. William of Tyre, pp. 7-8 and note 19 (manuscript V).
36. See note 34; William of Tyre, p.5, pp. 15-16 and pp. 17-18 (cf. *Editing William of Tyre*, in *Sacris Erudiri* 27, 1984, p.463).

But let's go back to our starting-point. The use of modern catalogues, with their different systems and various ways of spelling names – not to mention those which lack indices, or those (such as Brussels', and Oxford's Bodleian's) in which the descriptions of manuscripts bear other signatures than the volumes themselves – may not always be easy, but medieval catalogues, though a most important source, often make really treacherous reading, and you may find that instead of (e.g.) pointing to pieces by the censorious poet Gillebert[37], the listing *Cantica Gilleberti* stands for the prolific commentary on the Cantica Canticorum, the Song of Songs, by the 12th century English theologian Gilbert of Hoyland[38]. But if you do find your text mentioned in a medieval catalogue, it may be possible to figure out where the manuscripts of that particular monastery are now located, and whether the one you are looking for has even survived. If it has, and it can be established that it originated[39] from a centre well-known for its learning, then this may also explain certain readings, since the chances are that scribes in such a place were more capable of, and/or inclined to, intervene in the texts

37. *Serta*, pp. 685-762.
38. *Latomus* 17, 1958, pp. 541-542.
39. The distinction between origin and provenance is important: a manuscript's origin is the place where it was written, its provenance, the library it can be traced to. See also pp. 65-66, and *Serta*, p. 695, note 15.

they were copying than their colleagues in less sophisticated places[40].

Avoid making an edition from microfilms or microfiches only: these you may use to verify, but not as the basis on which to publish texts. Always use photocopies, preferably direct ones of the manuscripts themselves and not just enlarged from microfilms, on which you can make notes; and in any case, always see the originals before you consider your work done. Personal inspection usually yields – often substantial – results, especially in the case of less well-legible manuscripts, since it enables you to make a thorough check of your collations. But even if you collated a manuscript itself, also have a microfilm or photocopies made or put at your disposal: questions, unforeseen at the time, are bound to arise later on, and this way you will be able to verify readings at home.

Now , if you wish to publish just one single text in your whole life, then take your time. Even if your goals are less modest, never hurry, and, as I have already stressed, don't prepare more than one edition at a time. Since the tedious task of collating the

40. Comparable caution is indicated in the case of indirect traditions: since such quotations were made for well-defined reasons, one should be careful in evaluating variant readings from such sources – especially so if the texts are printed in less reliable editions or from unverifiable manuscripts.

same text in more than one manuscript will inevitably lessen your attention in the long, and not infrequently even in the short run, always verify every variant against the text of all manuscripts, and all manuscripts against every previously noted reading: the absence of a variant from your collations is no proof that you did not overlook it in one or more of your manuscripts. It is immaterial whether the text you use to collate your manuscript(s) against is printed or not. If several editions exist, use the least satisfactory one, your manuscript(s) will subsequently have more surprises in store for you, whereas collating against a good edition may well lull you into some inattentiveness. Although collating is undoubtedly a dull part of the work, what is transmitted by your manuscripts has to be your point of departure. They are not your Gospel, not even their consensus is, but you do have to start from what they transmit, and sloppy and thus unreliable collations are bound to result in unreliable editions.

If, in spite of my cautioning[41], you consider a manuscript to be an autograph, don't neglect the other manuscripts on that account. The original provides you with the text as it came out of the author's hands, or from under the author's eyes, but if the work had any influence at all, then its influence was almost certainly exerted, not by the autograph itself, but by

41. See pp. 18-20.

copies[42]. Therefore publish their readings as well! Also, in case you have been able to prove a manuscript to be the copy of another surviving manuscript, and thus possessing no independent value for the constitution of the text, still mention its most significant individual readings (or omissions) somewhere, not only because they may turn up in quotations or other forms of indirect tradition, but also because additional evidence may turn up which in its turn depends on this particular copy. The transmission of a text is a complex and not infrequently obscure matter, and the editor should not shrink from dealing with all such aspects. Do at least try to collate all the manuscripts you have been able to find. They may actually be too numerous to do so, and collating a very large number of manuscripts may not even add much to the results of collating only some of them. In such cases take test samples, a thing you can of course only begin doing after you have already got a clear idea about which readings are indeed relevant enough to be taken as samples. Never reject a manuscript merely on the basis of statements by others – you may well be in for a pleasant surprise if you don't[43]. And never consider more recent manuscripts as necessarily inferior to older ones. At the beginning of a

42. Cf. Guibert of Nogent, *Dei gesta per Francos*, p. 16/17 (the abbreviated text of the K-group). See also below, p. 39.
43. William of Tyre, pp. 8 and 11-13 (manuscript V); *Serta*, p. 803 (manuscript O).

manuscript tradition there may have been an igno-
rant, or absent-minded, or uninterested, or vindictive
scribe, or simply one shivering in some unheated
scriptorium, who produced a bad text, which may
have become the ancestor of others, whereas a century or more later a more gifted or scrupulous copyist may have produced a very reliable copy indeed.

Always pay the greatest attention to the orthography of such manuscripts as may have preserved the
author's own way of spelling. To be sure, many words
and proper names were written in more than one way,
and whatever system we adopt, it will always be too
rigorous. Realizing this does not dispense from dealing with this problem. Here too it is quite often possible to grasp, if not the details, at least the main lines.
An author who as a rule writes *ae* may well spell *esti-
mare, Cesar* or *Egidius*. One who used different sources
may well have borrowed different spellings from his
models, even for identical words. Did he write *extem-
plo* or *extimplo, a longe* or *alonge*[44], *postridie* or *post
tridie*[45], or distinguish *pignera* (relics) from *pignora*
(children)[46]? Some authors were certainly more old-
fashioned than others, some had a tendency to assimi-
late (*amm-, imm-*), others to dissimilate (*adm-, inm-*).
A sophisticated author like William of Tyre wrote obso-

---

44. *Serta*, p. 402, critical apparatus on line 404.
45. *Dei gesta per Francos*, p. 63.
46. Guibert of Nogent, *De pigneribus*, p. 15, note 11; *Dei gesta
    per Francos* 1, 82, note.

lete forms like *sequutus* and *exsequutor* as late as the second half of the 12th century, when hardly anybody would have dreamed of using such peculiar spellings. All such features should be carefully accounted for in your introduction; in isolated cases, e.g. if you print forms as the ones just mentioned, or perhaps ones like *coelum, foedus* or *moenia* in a later medieval Latin text, justify such spellings specifically. Although matters of orthography should be banned from your critical apparatus (I will deal with this later), in these particular cases you do have to include them (...*sic*...) to avoid confusion on the part of knowledgeable readers who may well suspect you of reproducing some 17th or 18th century edition rather than your manuscript(s). Often the only solution may be to mildly normalize the spelling of your text, or to simply follow one manuscript. But don't think of publishing a medieval Latin text as if it were a thousand years older[47]. If you were to dress up a classical author in the orthography of its medieval manuscripts you would be considered a fool and at the very least cause an indignant outcry, and quite rightly so; yet to use the reverse disguise for medieval authors – printing their works in classical spellings they never used – is still something considered quite acceptable by far too many.

When you have finished collating your manuscripts and selecting the variants you are going to

47. Or several centuries younger: *La tradition manuscrite de Guibert de Nogent*, pp. 21-22, note 15 !

mention in the critical apparatus, there remain two more things to be done: to make an analysis of the various readings, and to draw up a stemma. I take the view that sifting through the mass of readings is particularly important. In short texts this will hardly be necessary because it is so much easier to have a clear picture of the nature of the variants. But this is not the case with long texts, where the recurrence of certain readings, or certain types of readings, at longer intervals, will more often than not escape the attention; but put together and analysed they may well reveal a system, or a habit, whether good or bad, characteristic of the author or of (part of) the manuscript tradition, which is always important to be identified. This way you may discover, to give just one example, that the use of consecutive *ut* with an indicative, instead of, or along with, the subjunctive, far from being a scribal error, the frequency of which may not even have become apparent while collating the manuscripts and drawing up the critical apparatus, is actually a characteristic element of the author's style[48]. This way you will also avoid the dangerous

---

48. I am speaking here in particular of William of Tyre (p. 31). Until quite recently no one realized how much liberty this accomplished writer allowed himself, since all constructions which were not strictly according to what was commonly perceived as classical norms had been corrected away in previous editions: see the Introduction to his Chronicle, pp. 39-72: "Langue et style". – See also *Serta*, p. 546, relating to James of Vitry, *Ep.* 6,212-214, or *Peregrinationes tres*, p. 21.

possibility that philologists will be more interested in your (un)critical apparatus than in your text.

The second thing to do, if it is at all possible, is to present your readers with a stemma, which is nothing more than the graphical summing-up of the structure of the manuscript tradition as established in the introduction, the mutual relationship between the manuscripts you were able to examine and upon which you have based the constitution of the text. A stemma is basically built up by comparing the readings of (groups of) manuscripts which are not copies of one another: if these manuscripts have really significant readings in common which distinguish them from others, while at the same time sharing certain readings with these other manuscripts, then they must ultimately have a common ancestor, usually not preserved or not yet discovered, either remote or close, from which they have taken over readings and any such errors as have not already been corrected in the process of the manuscript transmission, and to which they have added other readings of their own. In this way you may well be able to show, at least roughly, the pedigree of all, or of most of, the manuscripts you have examined. Sometimes the discovery of one or more additional manuscript(s) changes the structure of the stemma, and thus may even necessitate a revision of the edition itself. This fact should not be considered surprising, nor be used as an argument against this method, since the stemma is like a snapshot, and an edition cannot possibly be based on more than the sum of resources available at the time of its publication. Neither the presence of a stemma, nor its absence, are in themselves indicative of an editor's or his edition's qualities or deficiencies. The stemma summarizes many, often long, pages of your introduction – though I'm inclined to say that the more complicated your argumentation, the less likely its outcome will be convincing. This certainly does not imply that the reader, after examining your stemma, should feel dispensed of reading the introduction, but you do render him a service by showing at a glance what it took you a lot of words to prove, e.g. that a whole branch of the manuscript tradition may be represented by no more than one single copy, and that the place this manuscript occupies in the structure of the tradition of the text renders it, by itself, as authoritative as all the others which together form just one other branch. Try to keep your stemma as simple as possible: few displays of learning are as ostentatiously academic as discussions about stemmas. Only take really relevant readings into consideration, and not such as may have been introduced by different scribes independently of the text of their models[49]. Hypothetical constructions and conclusions based on no more than a few isolated readings should be avoided in order to enable the reader to see the essential components. Many

49. See also p. 42.

complex manuscript traditions are more or less contaminated[50], which means that elements which should normally distinguish one branch from another are now inexplicably found in both, and in these particular cases separating the corn from the chaff is more than ever determined by the quality of the variants themselves. But in such cases too it usually remains possible to draw up a stemma, though details may be foggy and the constitution of the text will require even more skills from the editor.

Now the moment has arrived to give the text its definitive form. Exactly what are you going to publish? A critical edition? Or are you going to make light of your responsibility as an editor by procuring an edition based, on principle, upon just one single manuscript, whether a crudely diplomatic edition or one slightly more refined? Are you to follow Lachmann, Bédier, or Dom Quentin? You will find their theories and their methods described in treatises on textual criticism like the ones I mentioned at the beginning of this booklet. Personally I am all in favour of critical editions, for which Karl Lachmann (1793 – 1851) has set a shining example, even though he should of course never be considered a substitution for one's

50. I am referring to contamination between readings; contamination between versions [below, p. 38] is an altogether different problem, cf. Lena Wahlgren, *The Letter Collections of Peter of Blois*, Göteborg 1993, pp.102 and 104.

own experience and common sense. Dom Quentin's method was devised for the edition of the Vetus Latina, the pre-Hieronymian biblical texts, with all the particular problems they presented, and Bédier's was a reaction against the tendency of stemmas to have no more than two branches, thus allowing editors a free choice between variants, a tendency he, as a Romanist, first observed in editions of Old-French- , and subsequently of Latin texts, and of which he grew deeply, and unreasonably, suspicious. I don't know whether Dom Quentin's method ever proved to be a success even when applied by himself, but it did not really survive its learned initiator, as Bédier's did. Let me tell you about my own experience as an editor of critical editions, i.e. of editions which, by using as rich a manuscript tradition as possible and by critically evaluating the value of its various branches and readings, try to trace the text as far back as possible – which is not the same as to its origin: the author[51]. Three decades ago, in response to criticism and questions, I conducted a highly interesting seminar which aimed at putting the three above mentioned methods to the test. I chose the Chronicle of Sigebert of Gembloux and put photocopies of the autographical part of it in a sealed envelope. We then attempted to reconstruct the text by only using copies. Our procedure aimed at estab-

51. See p. 39.

lishing the text according to what I'll roughly call Lachmann's, Quentin's and Bédier's methods, and we concluded by comparing the results between them, and with the autograph. In a number of passages it proved altogether impossible to reconstruct the original text as the autograph finally revealed it to be, although this was not always due to methodical errors we had committed but could well have avoided. Otherwise, 'Lachmann's method' proved to be by far the most satisfactory one. You should, of course, be aware of the probability that even the original itself may have contained variant readings, and even errors, which then went on to lead an independent existence, thereby complicating the already sufficiently difficult task of the editor. But as long as you cannot ascertain that the original itself already contained a corruption, you have to assume it crept in later, and give the author the benefit of the doubt, because he himself would have most probably eliminated the error had he noticed it or recognized it as a mistake. *Letters* may have been sent simultaneously to several addressees, thus accounting for variants in otherwise largely identical originals[52]. Or an author may have published his work more than once, making alterations from one issue to another. In these circumstances we'll usually edit the final version and distinguish its text from that of the earlier one(s). The

52. *Serta*, p. 532.

textual quality of the manuscript(s) of the final version may nevertheless be inferior to that of the manuscript(s) of the earlier version(s)[53]; and in the case of passages where the author did not make any changes at all, no different versions exist either, and in these instances you'll have to base your text on all the available manuscripts, not just on those of the last 'edition' alone[54].

Even if you try to reconstruct the oldest attainable stage of the manuscript tradition, which should be your aim[55], you must nevertheless be aware of the fact that, as I have already mentioned[56], the original itself played much less important a role, if any at all, than its often defective descendants. Probably the most famous fake to have conquered medieval minds was the *Constitutum Constantini*[57], of which the textual quality of the version that really mattered was, from an editor's point of view, one of the worst.

53. This, for instance, is the case with one of Peter of Blois' Crusading treatises, the *Passio Reginaldi principis*, of which I am currently preparing an edition.
54. For a more or less comparable methodical error I committed in the first edition of the Letters of James of Vitry (1960), but corrected in the second one (2000), see *Serta*, p. 533. N.B. What looks like a version due to the author may in fact be no more than a text enlarged or abbreviated in the course of the manuscript tradition: *Serta*, pp. 169-175.
55. See p. 37.
56. See pp. 29-30.
57. Ed. Horst Fuhrmann, *Fontes iuris Germanici antiqui in usum scholarum*, X, 1968.

At all times, authors have sought to add words of their own invention to the existing vocabulary[58]. Decidedly *not* such a neologism was the word *bombones* or *bombonos* in a 12th century manuscript, in which the delighted editor thought to have discovered the very first mention of pralines: *"bombonos comedunt*, dit le prédicateur en parlant des écoliers" – when in fact the correct quotation should have been: *bombones comedunt apum labores* ("the drones devour what the bees slaved together") ...[59]

Now let us consider the very notion of errors and corrigenda as well as a few other obstacles the editor sees himself confronted with. A conscientious editor will weigh the readings of his manuscript(s) very carefully indeed, keeping in mind Quintilian's warning (9,4,39): *(quae) in veteribus libris reperta mutare imperiti solent, et dum librariorum insectari volunt inscientiam, suam confitentur.* Where no variants exist, the text may still have to be corrected; but where they do, making a choice between alternatives implies considering many, often quite different, aspects. Scribal errors are, of course, just what they are. However, a manuscript with many such errors is not necessarily a bad witness, but may well be an important witness copied by a bad scribe. Since most errors look easily recognizable, let's consider those readings

---

58. See pp. 17 and 46-47.
59. L.Traube, *Archiv für lateinische Lexikographie* 6, 1889, pp. 167-168 = *Kleine Schriften*, 1920, pp. 207-208.

which in spite of their appearance should not be corrected and may even have to be preferred for reasons that do not immediately meet the eye.

First of all: never lose sight of what kind of an author you are dealing with, and of the public his writing was intended to reach. In Petronius' *Cena* (48,4), the intoxicated braggart Trimalchio boasts: *et ne me putes studia fastiditum*: tres *bybliothecas habeo, unam Graecam, alteram Latinam*. I would have no qualms at maintaining this reading of the unique manuscript, instead of adopting the insipid correction *II bybliothecas* found in modern editions...[60]

There are quite a number of factual, and even grammatical errors the editor should not correct, since it is by no means certain that the author himself cannot have made them, or that he would have noticed them in a copy of his work[61] (of course, such readings must be acknowledged in the introduction and/or the apparatus). William of Tyre quotes Ovid's Heroïdes as *Naso noster*[62] *in libro ... Heroum* (16, 24, 8-9). In the Middle Ages, the work was fairly commonly called *Ovidius Epistolarum*[63], and we still ignore its original title: so don't let the title *we* give the work cause you to correct a medieval one by

60. Ed. Smith (Oxford 1975), Mueller (Teubner, 1995), following Buecheler (1862).
61. See also p. 17.
62. See above, note 17.
63. See the note on William of Tyre, p. 749,9 ; also *Accessus ad auctores*, p. 31, 19-22.

printing *Hero<id>um*. Adelman of Liège, speaking about his stay in the German town of Speyer, mentions *non solum Latinas, verum etiam Teutonicas aures, inter* quos *iam diu peregrinor*[64]. Several manuscripts present *(aures...) quas*. Quite apart from the fact that "peregrinari inter aures" is an improbable formula, it is clear that *Teutonicas* here stands for *Teutonicorum*; and since the "correction" *quas* could easily be made by whoever knew his Latin grammar, the reading has no relevance for a stemma[65]. The pilgrim Theoderic mentions the *montana Effraim*, qui *vocantur Sophim*[66], where he clearly had in mind both *montana* and *montes* (so in lines 1262-1263: *ista montana a modernis Belmont appellantur. Hiis montibus adiacet ...*). Guibert of Nogent, in his version of the *Gesta Francorum*, writes *ad dei cultum*, qua *illam imbuit*, the mistake being caused by the text of his model, which has *ad Christi culturam*[67]. Other such 'errors' which should remain the way they are, are found in quotations. Keep in mind that while we use – often excessively- normalized and corrected editions, based on as many different manuscripts as were available, medieval writers more often than not had to make do with a single manuscript, maybe a faulty one at that. So do try to check the manuscript tradi-

64. *Serta*, p. 183, 42-43.
65. See pp. 34-36.
66. *Peregrinationes tres*, p. 21, note 13, and p. 184,1266.
67. *Dei gesta per Francos* 6,64.

tion of the quoted text as well, and if you find the same readings or textual errors there, don't change them, since the author of the text you are editing must have used a model from which he took the incriminated reading. In his *Dei gesta per Francos* (3,45) Guibert of Nogent quotes the epitaph of Robert Guiscard: *quem Ligures regem*, Roma, Lemannus *habet*. It is evident that the original inscription (now lost), before the elision of the *A* took place in some early transcription, presented *Roma, Alemannus*, and this was already surmised by a highly intelligent 12th century interpolator (manuscript K). But Guibert, who himself never saw the tomb, apparently used William of Malmesbury's *Gesta regum Anglorum* (3, 262), from where he copied the senseless reading *Lemannus*. In those same *Dei gesta per Francos* (7, 713-714) he wrongly identified biblical Emmaus, not with ancient Nicopolis but with Neapolis (Nablus), a mistake he reproduced from a manuscript of Bede's *In Lucam* (24, 13-14). In the quotation from Ovid's Heroïdes I mentioned above, William of Tyre (16,24,11) simply copied the – quite common – reading *(ad vada) Menandri* (instead of *Meandri*)[68] from his model. Both John of Würzburg and Theoderic speak of the city of *Chyneret (Cinereth) … quae et Tiberiadis* (instead of *Tiberias*) in a passage they both borrowed from Fretellus. Boeren's edition of this author has *Tyberias*, but the two pilgrims could not have made the very

68. See my note on p. 749,9 (above, note 63).

same mistake independently, if it had not already existed in more than one Fretellus manuscript – and so I steered clear of correcting the word[69]. These are mistakes medieval authors had no means of recognizing the way we have, and consequently such readings have to be carefully preserved.

But there may be other reasons as well for maintaining them. Idungus of Prüfening, who (also) wrote excellent Latin, quotes from ecclesiastical authors certain passages with readings he cannot have failed to recognize as corruptions. Respect for his sources, probably as much as the lack of better manuscripts, nevertheless made him adopt them as he found them[70]. In the *Reynardus Vulpes* (357-358), the badly printed incunable which is our only source for the text, presents: *illa natat qua parte magis* declinior *unda/labitur*[71]. All previous editions, including my own of 1967, correct *declivior*. The original reading should however be maintained, since in manuscripts

69. *Peregrinationes tres*, p. 107,679-680 and p. 192,1482. For the same reason, I should not have followed one of my two manuscripts by correcting *Martinianum* in *Martianum* and *literaturam* in *literam* in my edition (1970) of Conrad of Hirsau's *Dialogus super auctores*, pp. 15-16. I adopted the corrections of these blatant errors on the assumption that Conrad would have made them himself if he had been able to revise his work. But since it is apparent that, for whatever reason, he was not (see also note 79), I should not have done so.
70. *Dialogus duorum monachorum*, pp. (11-) 13 and note 22.
71. *Serta*, p. 839.

of, and glosses on[72], Lucan (4,427), the passage's obvious model, both readings occur, and if the 1988 edition (by D.R. Shackleton Bailey) has *declivibus undis*, Housman's edition of 1927 presents *declinibus*: which at the same time teaches one not to rely solely on the most recent edition when it comes to verifying readings. In the *Metamorphosis Golie* (3, 4)[73], both manuscripts have *sed a pulsu melico tota resultabat*. This line is based on Martianus Capella (1, 11), where the Dick-Préaux edition (1978), p. 11,1, presents *melico quodam crepitabat appulsu*, but the critical apparatus duly registers a variant reading *a pulsu*[74].

72. *Adnotationes super Lucanum*, ed. Endt (Teubner, 1909), p. 140: *declinibus et declivibus*; Supplementum Adnotationum, ed. Cavajoni, 1979, vol. 1, p. 242: *declivibus*.

73. *Serta*, p. 805

74. (*apulsu* ed. Willis, 1983, p. 6,24, critical apparatus). – In the same *Metamorphosis Golie*, stanza 46 (*Serta*, p. 813), line 3 reads: *urit Apuleium* (five syllables) *sua Pudentilla*, where my two manuscripts have *Prudentilla* and *Pradentilla*. I have corrected these readings, since both sources for this line (Apuleius' *Apologia* and Apollinaris Sidonius) repeatedly mention *Pudentilla* without variants (edd. Butler-Owen, Oxford 1914, Helm (Teubner), 1959, and MGH, *AA* 8, 1887). On the other hand, in 43,2, *Zeno ponderabat*, I have maintained this name the way both manuscripts have it, instead of correcting *Zeto* (Sidonius) or *Zetus* (Isidore, *Etym.* 3,16,1, among the *inventores musicae*), a completely unknown person for whom the poet probably substituted the well-known philosopher (cf. also 43,1 *T(h)ales*, 2 *C(h)risippus*, 3 *Eraclius*, 4 *Samius* = Pythagoras).

Similarly, *indisparabiliter*[75] is a word one would be hard pressed to find in any dictionary; but it should not be corrected to *indispar*(or *per*)*tibiliter*, since the Thesaurus Linguae Latinae (7,1205,6) mentions that this form is indeed found in several manuscripts. And one more example, this time from Guibert of Nogent's treatise on (the abuse of) relics: *quorum tanta nebulonitate concutimur...ut...catellanos...exuperent*[76]. The neologism[77] *nebulonitas* he created to define rascals (*nebulones*). The scribe who copied this passage did not recognize the word and instead wrote the existing, but in this context meaningless, word *nebulositas*, which was later changed back again by a corrector – a fact which in itself proves that the hand which wrote this passage was not that of Guibert himself[78]. The word *catellanos* is not really a neologism but rather a ἅπαξ, since Guibert took it from a manuscript of St Jerome's Letters (147,4), where the correct reading is *Atellanus*. Hilberg's critical apparatus, however, registers *catellanus* as an existing reading (CSEL 56, p. 320,22). This word is an evident corruption; Guibert cannot possibly have guessed its meaning, because it has none. But since he found it in a context which lent it a most unsavoury ring, he

75. Guibert of Nogent, *Contra iudaizantem et Iudeos* 1639-1640 (*Serta*, p. 370).
76. CCCM 127, pp. 29(c)-30 = I,398-401.
77. See also p. 40.
78. See note 23.

nevertheless adopted it to characterize people he despised.

Needless to add that in the text itself the editor should not supply information the author himself had intended to provide later on but for one reason or other failed to do before his text was copied. In the *Dialogus super auctores* of Conrad of Hirsau there are no less than three such passages[79]; in William of Tyre (22,22,87-88) a date has been left in abeyance: *mense Octobre,... die mensis*. But in some cases words were deliberately omitted, since the subject was perfectly clear to medieval readers. So don't print *<dominus>*, *<Christus>* and the like when you come across a quotation, both explicit and implicit, introduced by no more than *dicit, dixit*, etc. No need either to write *<episcopus>* when someone is only called *Acconensis, Parisiensis, Podiensis*, etc.

Summa summarum, don't be afraid to correct the text of your manuscript(s) where you feel the necessity[80], but avoid correcting the author himself. If you feel uneasy about the correctness of the text but have nothing better to propose, then express your doubts

79. (see also note 69) *Accessus ad auctores* etc. , p. 14: *de quo mentionem idem Ieronimus faciens in epistola ad...; floruit autem auctor iste temporibus...; floruit autem idem Homerus temporibus r(egis...?)*.
80. See Dag Norberg, *Au seuil du Moyen Age* II, 1998, p.221, note 17. Norberg's death (in 1996) meant the loss of one of the most important philologists Sweden ever produced.

and never print a text you don't really understand
without any kind of comment: many a reader may
think his or her knowledge is insufficient to understand such a passage, which is presented as if you
considered it perfectly sound. Doing so is dishonest,
and unwise too, since other more knowledgeable
readers may unmask you.

Not infrequently the editor sees himself confronted
with two readings, each of which is (based on) a quotation. At the very beginning of this booklet I quoted
Matthew 9, 12. The same idea is expressed in Mark
2, 17 and again in Luke 5, 31, each time in a somewhat different wording. What, if a scribe, who, we
may assume, knew all three passages, chose to
replace the original quotation by one of the two others? For lack of a criterium one may simply adopt the
longest version, or the reading of the manuscript(s)
one as a rule trusts most, but there is no guarantee
that this is necessarily the right choice. In Peter of
Blois' *Dialogus*[81], one of the two manuscripts presents
(*loqueris et laboras*) *in vacuum* (Isaiah 49,4 or Philipp.
2,16), the other *in vanum* (Ps. 126,1). In the second
of Gillebert's two poems, all three manuscripts (one,
B, early 13th century, the other two (VW) 15th century) read: *fac, dum* terra mollis *est, rotam circuire*,
but above *terra mollis*, the same hand that wrote the

---

81. *Serta*, pp. 395-396, lines 226-227. See also *Serta*, p. 805
   (*Metamorphosis Golie*) 1,3: *florigera/florifera*.

text in B has written: *molle lutum*[82]. Since *molle lutum*
stems from Persius (3,23), I consider *terra mollis*
(Sapientia 15,7) to be a replacement of the original
words, and most certainly as a *lectio facilior*[83]. But in
44,4 the exact opposite is the case: *iste flet tenacibus*
vinculis *astrictus*[84]. Here the manuscripts BW have
ungulis, B with *vel vinculis* written over it; V has only
vinculis, and this must be the original reading, taken
from Virgil's *Georgica* 4, 412: *tenacia vincla*. But if two
manuscripts or branches of the manuscript tradition
each present a fundamentally different text, and you
cannot find any criterium at all to justify the adoption
of one of the two, it may be better to simply repro-
duce both readings[85].

82. *Serta*, pp. 695 and 746 (25,3). – See also below, pp. 64-65.
83. The basic idea behind this term is, that a *lectio difficilior*
is more likely to be simplified into a *lectio facilior* than
the opposite, e.g. *infitiari* is more likely to become *negare*
than the opposite. Generally speaking this may be true, but
one should be aware of the trap hidden underneath this
apparently sensible principle: much nonsense has been
printed simply because some word or construction was less
common or correct than the alternative.
84. *Serta*, pp. 695 and 749 (44,4).
85. *Peregrinationes tres* (John of Würzburg), pp. 135, 137 and
138. For the tentative reconstruction of inscriptions which
have since disappeared, see pp. 26-27 (Theoderic 590-595).
The same Theoderic had a passion for crypts and the number of steps leading into them. Admittedly, a few more or
less do not really matter, but it is annoying not to be at all
able to check the figures in lines 634 (45 ms.V,15 ms.M) or
1040 (16 V, 12, 17 or just 7 M).

There are still a few more types of readings about which I want to add a word of caution. Especially when a text was tightly written, copyists were apt to divide words wrongly[86]. There are a few famous emendations of this sort of corruption, such as J. Scheffer's *ab asse crevit* for *abbas secrevit*[87] in Petronius' *Cena Trimalchionis* 43, 1, or by Theodor Mommsen, who surmised that for *prius (ab Urbis initiis repetendum existimavi)*, the proper reading should be *P(opuli) R(omani) ius*[88]. Because for medieval writers the Roman author A(ulus) Gellius was called Agellius, by correcting this particular reading an editor betrays his own ignorance. More such misreadings are possible: *a deo/adeo, e dictis/edictis, ex Templo/extemplo*[89], *inter qu(a)e/interque, ob iter/obiter, pro re/pror(a)e, sed erunt/sederunt*, etc. Equally fre-

---

86. See also p. 65.
87. In P. Burman's *ed.altera*, Amsterdam 1743, p. 262.
88. *Digesta* II,1: *De origine iuris.–* In the famous Codex Mediceus (49.9) (9th century), of Cicero's *Ad familiares* (4,13,2), the words *(his) quidem omnibus* have been corrupted to *qui demonibus* ! (This reading is not listed in the critical apparatus of modern editions, such as W.S. Watt, Oxford 1982, p. 124,13 or D.R. Shackleton Bailey (Teubner), 1988, p.121,13, but it is mentioned in R.Y. Tyrrell and L.C. Purser, *The Correspondence of M. Tullius Cicero*, IV, 1894, p. 485, adnotatio critica). And the pilgrim John of Würzburg (or a manuscript of his model Fretellus) created a place *Gerlicus* out of *Ger, locus...* (*Peregrinationes tres*, p. 19 = p. 98,484).
89. *Peregrinationes tres*, p. 157, 465.

quent are malformations of the type *contenti/contempti, correptio/correctio, credulitas/crudelitas, exanimare/examinare, fame/fama*[90], *fata/facta, frusta/frustra, ministerium/misterium*[91], *pravitas/parvitas, revelare /relevare, sinibus/finibus, suspicere/ suscipere*, errors caused by misinterpretation of abbreviations and contractions like *causa/eam, cum/tamen, haec/autem, idem/ id est, spe(m) /specie*, or caused through pronunciation: *ac/hac, ortus/hortus, ostium/hostium*, etc. (this last category may simply be a question of orthography, in which case there is nothing wrong). The fact that a certain reading occurs more than once is no indication of either authenticity or scribal error: both author and copyist may well have been prone to repetition, especially in long texts, and an error remains an error, even when repeated. On the positive side, however, if you can detect a tendency to repeat the same formula, it may be wise to stick to it. Conrad of Hirsau, in (my edition of) his *Dialogus super auctores*, concludes his treatment of three writers as follows: *Sed de hoc auctore satis dictum* (316,1041-1042, and 1196-1197). But in the second of these passages, one of the two manuscripts has *satis* est *dictum*. Conrad might well have written *est* himself; but as long as the

90. William of Tyre 4, 21, 39 and Guibert of Nogent, *Dei gesta per Francos* 7,1787.
91. Berengar of Tours, *Rescriptum*, pp. 22-23.

editor cannot make this plausible, I recommend not to change what appears to be a stereotype[92].

If a passage proves to be corrupt beyond repair, just place a crux (†)[93], because you shouldn't try to make it readable at any cost: a critical edition is not a school textbook. A corruption may be much more serious than it looks at first sight[94]. E.g., if your manuscripts should present an obviously erroneous reading *transeuntibus*, and you can make the text flow smoothly by printing *transire*, don't be too proud of your correction. You may be right, of course; but don't let yourself be led into the temptation of making any such guess, unless you are able to explain how the simplest form of the verb could possibly become corrupted into one so much more complicated. In these cases I would rather assume that some part of the text has been lost, possibly, as is so often the case, because the scribe's eye strayed from one identical word or ending to another (*homoioteleuton*). That is the troub-

92. For the *cursus* as a criterium, see *Serta*, pp.380-381 (Peter of Blois), William of Tyre, p. 39, note 65, or Guibert of Nogent, *Dei gesta per Francos* 5,629 (critical apparatus). *Rhyme* is another criterium: if an author, whose prose is characterized by rhyme (e.g. Caesarius of Heisterbach: *Serta*, pp. 412-413), quotes Proverbs 27,6, he will be more likely to write *meliora sunt vulnera diligentis/quam fraudulenta oscula odientis* than... *odientis oscula*.
93. See p. 62.
94. See also p. 13.

le with editing: anything may have happened while the scribe was writing, this however does not mean that the editor should feel free to intervene in whatever way he likes. Now, making a correction, especially an important one: a conjecture, is just another way of confessing that you don't understand the text as it stands. But although you are sure the text is corrupt, you also think you know how to repair the damage. In this case, don't be afraid to show your skills! Often it is the seemingly minor correction of hardly perceptible corruptions which will establish, and maintain, your reputation as an editor. It has become fashionable to pour cheap scorn on the text critics of bygone centuries. To be sure, a considerable number of them went to any length to rewrite texts as if they had originally been written by themselves. But many of these same people nevertheless did make valuable contributions to learning. So tone down such criticism until you yourself have acquired their often phenomenal knowledge of Latin. Don't fall into the opposite trap either by printing just plain rubbish for lack of ability to deal with a difficult text and/or a defective manuscript tradition, an attitude not infrequently disguised as respect for the manuscripts. You may use readings from late and even from interpolated manuscripts[95], as long as you are aware of what

95. See the introduction to William of Tyre's Chronicle, pp. 22-31: "BW: une véritable édition médiévale de la Chronique".

you are doing: there is no reason to reject any correction on the implied grounds that it was made by someone other than yourself, and it is quite irrelevant whether a correction was made by a modern or by an anonymous medieval textual critic.

Understanding a printed text depends in no small measure on its punctuation. This is as important a subject as it is touchy, because editors tend to introduce their native habits into Latin texts. Don't scatter commas all over it, just keep together what belongs together, both grammatically and logically, instead of breaking up well-balanced phrases. Far from assisting the reader, too many commas only serve to obscure the structure of the phrase and the development of the thought. Pay attention to the punctuation of your manuscript(s)[96]. Whilst on the whole being unsuitable for modern readers[97], it may frequently provide the editor with a clue as to the author's intention, and, in the case of quotations, as

---

96. Do not misinterpret ~, which may be either our question-mark or the ending –ur. And do not overlook the signs ″ ″ (″dicit ″dominus = dominus dicit, see p. 62).

97. E.g., in R.W. Southern's edition of Eadmer's *Vita s. Anselmi* (London 1962), the introduction (pp. XXVIII-XXXIV) gives an excellent idea of a medieval system of punctuation, but reproduced in the text itself this system renders reading most difficult. Nothing good at all can be said of a similar attempt by J.H. and L.L. Hill, *Le "Liber"* (sic) *de Raymond d'Aguilers*, Paris 1969 : cf. William of Tyre, pp. 94-95.

to how he read and (mis)understood them[98]. Quite often I myself mention *sic distinxi cum codice* or *cum codicibus* in the critical apparatus[99]. In the well-known biblical phrase[100], the punctuation is crucial: *vox clamantis in deserto: parate viam domini* or *vox clamantis: in deserto parate viam domini.* In Guibert of Nogent's *Contra iudaizantem et Iudeos*, where Isaiah 9,6 is quoted, the manuscripts leave a choice between *deus fortis, pater (futuri seculi)..., deus, fortis, pater...* and *deus, fortis pater...*[101] The first verses of the *Reynardus Vulpes* are: *Fabula Reynardi, sicut reor agnita multis/teutonice scripta, metrificata sonet.* One would be printing nonsense by putting the comma otherwise:... *multis, teutonice scripta metrificata* (i.e. in Latin distichs) *sonet*[102]. In Bernard of

98. E.g. Guibert of Nogent, *Dei gesta per Francos* 7,803-805 or 1992-1993.
99. E.g. in Guibert of Nogent's *Contra iudaizantem et Iudeos* 1425-1426 (*Serta*, p. 363), where in a quotation from Jeremiah 31,33, I have followed my manuscripts by printing: *sed hoc erit pactum quod feriam cum domo Israel: post dies illos dabo legem meam*, but where editions of the Vulgate (Stuttgart 1975, p. 1211, and Rome (ed. Vaticana), 1979, p. 1376) read: . . . *cum domo Israel post dies illos, dicit dominus: dabo legem meam.* See also Guibert's *Dei gesta per Francos* 7,847-848, 1058-1059, 1100-1101, 1643-1644, etc.
100. Isaiah 40,3, Matthew 3,3, Mark 1,3 and Luke 3,4.
101. *Serta*, p. 332,485.
102. *Serta*, p. 828.

Utrecht's *Commentum in Theodolum* (245-248), he says: *de capris autem phisiologi aiunt quod frondibus, nunquam herba satiantur*[103]. The punctuation should be like this, although some manuscripts omit *nunquam* and others have *frondibus nunquam, herba sepe satiantur*: goats eat leaves, not grass. In Peter of Blois' *Dialogus*[104], the abbot tells the King: *sicut te habebis erga inimicum tuum, ita se habebit erga te qui te in sanguine suo de servo et inimico fecit filium et amicum*: if a comma had been put after *erga te*, the subject would not have been Christ (*qui... amicum*) but the King's enemy (*inimicum tuum*). In Guibert of Nogent's *Dei gesta per Francos* (3, 98-99) I printed: *Quod imperatoris qui inde non procul aberat dum comperisset exercitus...*, since the subject is the emperor's army, and not the emperor, who at that time was in Constantinople: by putting *qui... aberat* between commas one would have caused *himself* to be in the vicinity. And one more quotation from the same work (7, 1516-1518). A demon assures a knight about his master, the devil himself: *Cum enim sit liberalis nec desit opulentia infinita dandorum, affectantibus opes supra quam valeat estimari largus est munerum*. I followed the majority of my manuscripts here, instead of two of them (BeR) which wrote: *opulentia infinita, dandorum... munerum*.

---

103. Lines 719-720, pp. 103-104.
104. *Serta*, p. 392, 132-134.

A few more technicalities need considering. I recommend printing explicit quotations in *italics*, and
implicit ones in the same type as the rest of the text[105]
(naturally both have to be identified in the notes).
Whenever you have to divide a word, do it the right
way, don't write *manus-cript* but *manu-script, apo-sto-
lus, Chri-stus* and *Chri-stianus, epi-scopus*, and follow the rule that in Latin one transfers as many letters
to the next line as is allowed by the language: *co-
gnoscere, di-gnus, ma-gnus, no-ster, ve-ster*, etc.
Another point concerns the use of capitals. I myself
print *dominus* and *deus, christianus* as an adjective

105. I have also used italics for what are really implicit quotations, but which the author clearly assumed to be
recognized by saying: *sicut enim..., quia...*, and the like.
E.g., the *Epistola ad heremitas* (155, *Serta*, p. 222) reads:
qui adheret domino, unus spiritus est (1 Cor. 6,17). I have
printed these words in italics, since the author showed
it to be a quotation by concluding: *ergo qui non adheret...*,
etc. But I did not use italics for three implicit quotations
in Guibert of Nogent's *Dei gesta per Francos*, although
there can be no doubt at all that (here too) his readers
would have recognized the source: (2,355-356) *Licet enim
emulationem dei habere viderentur, sed non secundum scientiam...* and (4,848-849) *Emulationem quippe dei
habuerat, sed non secundum scientiam...* (Rom.10,2), or
(7,1647-1648) *Cum enim... ampullas et sesquipedalia
verba* (Horace, *Ars Poetica* 97) *proiciat...* In the *Reynardus
Vulpes* (1253, *Serta*, p. 867), a lonely spot is described as
desertus locus ille nimis, but the resemblance with
Matthew 14,15: *desertus est locus...* may well be a pure
coincidence.

but *Christianus* as a substantive. The same also applies to languages: *lingua latina* but *in Latino*. Likewise with saints, and the churches and monasteries which are under their patronage: *sanctus Iohannes* but *(a)ecclesia Sancti Iohannis*, and *dominicum sepulchrum* but *Dominicum Sepulchrum* if the church of the Holy Sepulchre is meant[106]. Names are of course printed with capitals, but it is not always easy to ascertain whether one is actually dealing with a profession or trade, or with a name (which at the same time may or may not indicate someone's own, or an ancestor's profession). In a text like the Chronicle of Vézelay, that splendid and once very rich Burgundian abbey, this problem arises quite frequently: *Blanchardus sartor* or *Sartor*? *Iohannes bergerius* or *Bergerius*? *Iohannes piscator* or *Piscator*? As in many cases the unique 12th century manuscript gave no clue at all, I, as often as it seemed reasonable, considered such adjectives as designations of profession or trade, not just because in twelfth-century Burgundy real family names were still rare, but also in order to preserve possible indications of economic activity[107].

106. *Peregrinationes tres*, pp. 32-33.
107. *Monumenta Vizeliacensia* (see also p. 69), p. XL and the General index under the heading "Métiers et fonctions" (pp. 661-662). See also J.F. Benton, *Consciousness of Self*, in (R.L. Benson and G. Constable) *Renaissance and Renewal in the Twelfth Century*, Oxford 1982, pp. 281ff.

Make sure that before you have your text printed, you translate it, even if you are not actually going to publish the translation. This is an indispensable check, if your text is to be unimpeachable. Glancing over it is easy enough, you should'nt fail to understand what it is all about. But it is a different matter altogether to have your text translated aloud, to have it put into your own language is a test which the Latin text you have established should truly stand up to. And even in this way one can still make mistakes. *Experto crede*: in his second Letter James of Vitry writes: *transivi... per locum ubi mulier Cananea post dominum clamans* et *de micis que cadunt de mensa dominorum suorum catulos edere... asseruit*[108]. It is easy to identify the implicit quotation: Matthew 15,27. In my first edition (1960) I however did not realize that *et* (also, even) is part and parcel of the quotation, and therefore translated it wrongly by *and*. But in this case a verb is missing, which I subsequently supplied by inserting *(clamans) <accurrit>*, a correction which nicely masked a serious mistake and which would not have been bad at all... if I had been right. However, translating does not merely mean knowing the Latin language well enough[109], it

108. *Serta*, p. 572, 354-357.
109. At a time when knowledge of Latin is dwindling, translators too should be careful not to discount St Matthew's warning (15, 14): *caecus si caeco ducatum praestet, ambo in foveam cadunt.* See p. 11 and notes 110, 115 and 123.

also entails using plain common sense. In the introduction to Guibert of Nogent's *Dei gesta per Francos*
(p. 22-23) I listed a number of serious mistakes made
in a 19th century translation[110]. I'll mention one of
them. The dedicatory letter to the bishop of Soissons
opens with the words: *Cum ab amicis michi sepe sug-
gereretur aliquibus, quare opusculum presens* proprio
non insignirem nomine... Guizot translated this with:
my name (mon nom). To be sure, the manuscripts
of the work did (and do) bear the name of the author!
What is meant, and should be evident, is *a*, namely
someone's, proper name, that is, the name of some
illustrious person (such as that bishop of Soissons),
the dedication to whom would lend additional lustre
to the work.

Under the Latin text there should be at least two
sets of notes, one explanatory and identifying quotations etc., the other, the critical apparatus, listing the
variants and containing all the various short remarks
you deem necessary to explain your constitution of
the text. The critical apparatus is an essential part
of the edition. What it should not contain are all such
readings as are irrelevant to the constitution of the
text: sub-variants and orthographica (with the pos-

110. Some of these, as well as many others, are also found in
R. Levine's English translation of this text (Woodbridge
1997, see my edition of the Latin text, p. 21, note 28,
and above, note 5). An elegant and reliable (French)
translation is that by Monique-Cécile Garand (Turnhout
1998).

sible exception of some proper names). Don't think half a page of variants permits a better control of your text than only a few lines may. The opposite is true: the more variants, the harder it becomes to use the critical apparatus. Certain readings, such as interpolations or marginal or interlinear readers' comments[111], may nevertheless still be important for whatever other reasons. In these cases you should discuss them in your introduction or in your explanatory notes, or list them in a second apparatus, in short, in a place where they are sufficiently in evidence so as not to escape the attention without being mistaken for relevant variants. The critical apparatus can be positive or negative, depending on the manuscript tradition. If it is simple, it is enough to mention only those readings which were not adopted into the text (*e.g.* servat] habet MP, or just: *habet* MP); if complicated (which is not necessarily the same as having been transmitted in numerous manuscripts), it is better to mention both, first the adopted reading, then the rejected one: *colliduntur* CEHG, *allidunt* MBS. If several manuscripts repeatedly present the same

111. James of Vitry, *Ep.* 6,279-291 (*Serta*, pp. 621-622), interpolations concerning St Francis of Assisi; *Dialogus duorum monachorum* 3,470, criticism of the Cistercians; *Serta*, p. 385(2); C.L. Grotefend, *Die Edelherren von Boldensele oder Boldensen*, Hanover 1855, p.31, note 1 (on the *tunica inconsutilis*) and p. 39, note 1; A.Wilmart, *Un lecteur ennemi d'Amalaire* [De officiis ecclesiasticis], *Revue Bénédictine* 36, 1924, pp. 317-329.

readings, it may well be practical to unburden the apparatus by grouping the sigla into a single one: α instead of CDM, β instead of PKV, etc.[112]. Always mention the names of the scholars who made the emendations you adopt or reject. Distinguish your own observations from the rest of the text by printing them in *italics*. Write your own interventions out in full (preferably in Latin): *addidi, conieci (coniecerim), correxi (correxerim), scripsi*, etc., those concerning others, persons and manuscripts alike, in an abbreviated form: *add.* (= addit, addidit, or the plural), *coni.* (coniecit), *corr.* (correxit), *del.* (delevit), *eras.* (erasit) (or *in rasura*), *exp.* (expunxit), *i.m.* (in margine), *m²* (manu(s) altera *or* alia), *om.* (omittit *or* omisit), ... *post*..., *pr.* (prius, i.e. before correction), *ss.* (supra adscripsit), *trp.* (transposuit, i.e. changed the order of the words concerned)[113]. In the text itself, the sign < > indicates the restitution by the editor of a lost part of the sentence, square brackets, words to be excluded from the text; a *crux* (†) signals a corruption deemed beyond repair[114], while asterisks (***) indicate that something is missing (in that case, if you wish to add an additional observation in the apparatus, it could read: *exciderunt quaedam* (or, a little

112. Ω or ω is used to indicate an archetype only. For *A*, see note 28.
113. See note 96.
114. See p. 52.

more cautiously: *quaedam excidisse videntur)* or *desiderantur quaedam* or *aliqua)*. But since I have seen too many cases of [...] being misunderstood[115], I came to drop that sign altogether, making a note in the apparatus instead (N.B.: editions of papyri and inscriptions make a different use of some of these signs).

The way you present the readings you decided to register in your critical apparatus is important too. Because interpreting someone else's apparatus is often hard enough for the specialist, make it as comprehensible as possible. Try to quote your manuscripts or groups of manuscripts consistently in the same order, and not now this way, now that way, if there is no need to do so. Let your critical appara-

---

115. Thus in ch. 7 of Master Gregory's *Narracio de mirabilibus urbis Rome*, where in my edition of 1970 the words *dimisso capite velut* (now [*Serta*, p. 287, 206] in the critical apparatus) were put between brackets. John Osborne, in his translation (Toronto 1987), completely ignored the signs and mis-translated accordingly (p.23). Apparently, this translator's knowledge of Latin was as shaky as that of R. Levine's (note 110). Two samples: *avisque a castris quantum clamor auditur appellantis* (91-92) does not mean "and while the loud cry of a bird could be heard coming from the camp" (p.20) but "and as far from the camp as one can hear the cry of a bird that calls out... "; and in ch. 12, lines 283-284, the words *(propter...) nescio quam magicam persuasionem* do not mean "some magic spell that I'm unaware of" (p.26) but "some inexplicable magic spell". *Sapienti sat.*

tus always serve to explain really what happened in the course of the transmission of the text. E.g., in the *Dialogus duorum monachorum* certain words have been glossed in certain manuscripts, and these explanations gradually came to lead a life of their own, sometimes driving out and replacing the original readings[116]. The critical apparatus should clearly show a development of this kind: (1,83) *Veritas* HL, *Veritas* with gloss *Christus* Z, *Veritas Christus* AM; (2, 282) *temerariae* with gloss *vel precipiti* MZ, *temerariae vel (sive) precipiti* AL, *precipiti* only H; (2,693) *Norbertini* HMZ, with gloss *quidam* M, *quidam Norbertini* AL; (3, 816) MONAXOI (M, corrupted to NOMAXOI HZ) with gloss *monachi* HMZ, *monachi* only AL; (3, 820) *eiusdem regulae scriptor* HL and with gloss *Augustinus* MZ,... *scriptor Augustinus* A. A few more examples, this time from Guibert of Nogent's *Dei gesta per Francos*[117]: (5, 590) *ipsos* α (= the group of manuscripts FG^{2}K), *eos* B^{2}R, *vel ipsos eos* BeGG^1; (6, 23) *spectaculo*] *vel miraculo* gloss in K, *miraculo* G^2; (7, 1525) *voluntati* K, R and the group BeGG^1, *voluntati* with gloss *vel pro velle* B^2, *vel pro velle voluntati* G^2, *pro velle* only F; (7,1874) *nos opulenter* αG^1, *nos opulenter nos* R, BeG and the model of B^2, which manuscript sought to correct the obvious error but suppressed the wrong

---

116. See also pp. 48-49.
117. For two particularly interesting marginalia which crept into the text proper of that work, see the Introduction, pp. 52-53.

word , writing *opulenter nos*; (7, 2077-2078)[118] *ad extera* FKB², *a dextera* R, *ad dextera* BeGG¹, *ad dexteram* G², etc.

As for the explanatory notes, they should help the reader and contain all kinds of useful information on the wording and the contents of the text, but keep in mind an edition is only the starting point for research. Your work should aim at being the last word in editing; it need not be an attempt at making subsequent study of the subject of the text superfluous.

There are two more, very important parts of any edition to be discussed, viz. the introduction, and the indexes and concordances. In spite of the often considerable intellectual efforts that go into it, the introduction is likely to be the least used part of any edition, especially if the Latin text has the good fortune of becoming the basis for further research, and its editor one whom people acknowledge as being reliable (this last circumstance may well put a serious strain on the editor's self-criticism). Still, although one should keep the introduction concise and factual, it should deal, as much as possible and necessary, with the author, the work itself, its place within the whole of the author's production and the influence it may have exercised; above all, it should provide a description of the manuscript(s) and trace its, or their, provenance and origin[119]. Very useful in this respect

118. See p. 50.
119. See p. 26 and note 39.

are medieval catalogues of libraries (above, p. 27) and early works such as the *Voyage littéraire de deux Bénédictins*, undertaken at a time when many manuscripts were still in monastic or other ecclesiastical libraries[120], Dom Bernard de Montfaucon's *Bibliotheca Bibliothecarum* (1739), or the *Bibliotheca Latina* (1734-1736/1858-1859) by J.A. Fabricius, a scholar who used his own collection of manuscripts, which were auctioned off after his death[121]. You should subsequently deal with your manuscripts' textual qualities and deficiencies and their mutual relationship, and also with their material aspects and the use you have been able to make of them. It should be evident that you have to extract as much, and as varied, information from it as possible, but in an edition

120. This was not always a guarantee, though: wanting to study the manuscripts of the Sainte-Chapelle in Bourges, in August 1708, "je les trouvai dans un état pitoyable, parce que le receveur du chapitre, à qui on avoit confié la clef de ce lieu, en avoit fait un poullalier (*sic*); et que comme ils étoient sur des pupitres, les poules les avoient couverts d'ordures" (Dom Edmond Martène, *Voyage littéraire de deux Bénédictins* I,1717,p.29); *Serta*, p. 157, note 6: "On m'avoit assuré qu'il y avoit environ trente ans [*ca.* 1730], on avoit été obligé de jetter dans la Loire des tombereaux entiers de livres de cette église [Saint-Martin of Tours], pourris par l'humidité du lieu peu fréquenté où ils avoient été placés . . .".

121. *La tradition manuscrite de Guibert de Nogent*, pp. 33-35; *Dei gesta per Francos*, pp. 29-31.

the manuscripts are not studied for their own sake: they were made to transmit a text, and it is that text the editor is ultimately after, and so are his readers. So don't accumulate all kinds of material details that are irrelevant in this context: that's for codicologists to indulge in. Draw up the stemma; study the Latin and matters of orthography; list and discuss earlier editions, and whatever else may be important or interesting. Try to persuade your publisher to add one or more reproductions of important manuscripts: they'll provide the reader with information no words can convey, and they'll break the monotony of so many pages of black print. And although you are of course sure not to have overlooked any readings – no matter whether in the end you mention them in your critical apparatus or not – do collate the reproduced page(s) an additional time. If your readers make a check and discover an error, you will never manage to persuade anyone that by the most extraordinary of chances this was precisely the only stitch you dropped.

And finally the last part of the edition. No work should ever be allowed to appear without carefully worked-out indexes (and concordances, if need be). The better they make the text accessible, the greater the service you render your readers. Here too the utmost care should be taken: few things infuriate as much as looking something up and consequently being frustrated because the reference was not correct. Don't be too rigid in your system, an index is not an exercise in strict logic but a means of assistance: as long as it works optimally, stick to it, but since no system, however sophisticated, is likely to work one hundred percent of the time, just change it in the few particular cases where you feel the need. Although the number of indexes should depend on the kind of edition, there are rarely too many. Usually a Biblical index and one of authors and texts, quoted or alluded to, will be useful. So is an index of all passages mentioned or discussed in the introduction: people may wish to examine your reasons for (not) adopting a particular reading, about which the critical apparatus, being necessarily concise, can provide only an outline. If documents are inserted in the text, do add a list of their incipits. The General index should not only comprise proper names, but also various functions, notions of money and prices, etc., in short, whatever information will facilitate the reader's research. Often a person or town are named so many times that you have to restrict yourself to mentioning only the most interesting passages ("and *passim*"). But if one only lists their proper names, important implicit references will inevitably escape the user of the index, so they too should be noted: if, quite outside the chronological framework within which the reader is looking, it is said that (un)like someone's (grand-)father or (grand-)son such or such a person was... (cruel, generous, mean, bald: whatever), be sure to include such passages under both proper names, lest the information they contain should be lost. Queen Melisende of Jerusalem is quite frequently mentioned in William of Tyre's Chronicle, but since we know nothing about her physical appearance, my index (p. 1139) specifically indicates a passage in which she is implicitely described as being thin[122]. And in the Cartulary and the Chronicle of Vézelay[123] so many different people and places are mentioned, that I decided to list them, not just under their proper names, but also under those of their families (fathers, mothers) , villages and towns, in order that such sociologically and economically important information may become more readily available[124].

And last but not least: all the efforts you invest in your work come to very little if you don't correct your proofs the way you should: so that no misprints deface your pages and hideously stare your readers in the face[125]. To be sure, there are misprints and misprints.

122. ... *nec matris exemplo dici posset* [King Baldwin III] *macilentus* (16, 1, 23-24).
123. *Monumenta Vizeliacensia*, CCCM 42 (and Supplementum, 1980). Excellent translation by John O.Ward and John Scott, *Hugh of Poitiers, The Vézelay Chronicle*, New York 1992.
124. See also p. 58.
125. In one of the many volumes of the *Analecta Hymnica* (44, 1904, p. 10), the editor Clemens Blume signals the error *liturgische Possen* ("liturgical pranks", instead of *Prosen*: sequences), occurring not less than three times in the *Jahresberichte der Geschichtswissenschaft*.

In a (spurious?) letter, Erasmus complains about a particularly dirty trick one of his printers played upon him in his *De vidua christiana*, dedicated to Mary Queen of Hungary, by printing *mentula* (= penis) instead of *mente illa*[126]. No copy with the incriminated word has ever been found, so the passage may well have been expurgated in time. The same is not true of two typographical 'errors' made during the reign of the Emperor Napoleon III (1852-1870). They are found in the Moniteur, the official gazette of the regime. In a bulletin on the precarious health of old Jerome, ex-King of Westphalia and uncle of the Emperor, someone, instead of printing "le *mieux* persiste" (the improvement continues), printed " le *vieux* persiste" (the old one hangs on), and another time, describing the Empress's dress, he printed, not "souliers de *satin*" (satin shoes) but "souliers de *catin*" (a whore's shoes)[127]. Rebellious French compositors seem to have had a certain inclination to draw from that sort of vocabulary, since Mussolini's son-in-law and Minister of Foreign Affairs, count Ciano, mentions in his Diary[128] that an opponent of the Vichy gov-

---

126. H.M. Allen-H.W. Garrod, *Opus epistolarum Des. Erasmi* XI, 1947, p. 360,83-94. Cf. V. Tourneur, *Bibliotheca Erasmiana*, Brussels 1936, pp.200-207.

127. J. Carcopino, *Les bonnes leçons*, Paris 1968, p. VII.

128. Ed. M. Muggeridge, London 1947, p.462 (April 29,1942).

ernment got himself into hot water with the author-
ities by printing, not (the Marshal) Pétain but *Putain*
(Whore)... On a loftier level, I am perfectly aware of
the story that it was a printer's error that lent additional grace to one of the most beautiful stanzas of
Malherbe[129], and that another immortalized the last
quarter of an hour of the life of the Marshal de La
Palisse[130]. But in editing medieval Latin texts, where
it is not even always evident whether one is dealing
with an error or an idiosyncracy, it is absolutely necessary to avoid this kind of confusion. Make sure you
build up a reputation, not only as a gifted textual
critic, but also as a meticulous and reliable one - then,
even though from time to time readers are bound to
challenge your conclusions, they will continue to
respect you – professionally that is – and put trust in
your texts, and even the occasional misprint, which
resisted all your efforts to avoid it, will then more easily be condoned. And one final warning: should you
wish to dedicate your work to someone, be careful

129. *Consolation à M. du Périer*, lines 13-16: "Mais elle était
     du monde, où les plus belles choses/ont le pire destin/
     et *rose, elle* [Rosette-Roselle] a vécu ce que vivent les
     roses/ l'espace d'un matin".
130. "Un quart d'heure avant sa mort [in the battle of Pavia,
     24 February 1525] il était encore en vie" (*instead of*: il
     faisait encore envie).

not to make a fool of yourself by printing rubbish such as this incredible one: *Ad Mater Meum*[131].

And now, if you are not discouraged by the fact that all the above represents no more than a sketch of a long and arduous process, do embark upon this wonderful career as an editor of medieval Latin texts. There is still much to be done, and in the words of St Matthew (9,37) and St Luke (10,2), the harvest is abundant enough, but the labourers are few.

131. A.F. Ide, *Calendar of Death: Socio-Psychological Factors in Thomas of Canterbury's Attitude Toward His Own Death*, Scholars Books, Irving (Texas), 1986 (with thanks to Professor P.G. Schmidt, himself a distinguished editor, who brought this pearl to my attention. I also owe thanks to Professor Peter Ganz, whose expert opinion I sought and who I feel honoured to say accorded me his *imprimatur*).

INDEX OF POST-MEDIEVAL PROPER NAMES

SUBJECT INDEX

The present edition of this book has been typeset
in Walbaum and printed by Drukkerij De Windroos,
Beernem, Belgium, on Free Life Vellum paper
in December 2000.